Tiny Gold Dress

Other books from Lunar Chandelier Press

Radio at Night by Laurie Price [forthcoming]
Earth after Earth by Toni Simon,
with drawings by the author 2012
Deliberate Proof by Vyt Bakaitis 2010
petals, emblems by Lynn Behrendt 2010
Homework by Joe Elliot 2010

Tiny Gold Dress

John Godfrey

For Jack Kimball
With high regard

JGodfrey
21 X 13

LUNAR CHANDELIER PRESS

ISBN: 978-0-9846076-4-8

The author thanks the Foundation for Contemporary Arts for
the generous fellowship that enabled the writing of these works.

Some of these poems have appeared in *Brawling Pigeon*, *Gerry Mulligan*, *Mimeo
Mimeo*, *The Poetry Project Newsletter*, *Live Mag!*, *The Nation* and *VLAK*.

"Tiny Gold Dress" first appeared as a broadside produced by Ugly Duckling
Presse to benefit The Poetry Project on the occasion of its 45th anniversary (2010).

"Start of the Ball" appeared in the catalogue for an exhibition, "Inner Visions,"
curated by Alex Katz from works in the permanent collection of the
Colby College Museum of Art, Waterville, Maine, in July 2012.

Cover image by Basil King © 2012 Courtesy the artist www.basilking.net
From the series: "Tiny Gold Dress" 30" x 22" Sharpie Permanent Marker

Book and cover design by Julie Harrison www.julie-harrison.com
Photo credit: cover and author by Ani Berberian

Published by Lunar Chandelier Press
Brooklyn, New York 11201
www.lunarchandelier.com
lunarchandelier@gmail.com

 LUNAR CHANDELIER PRESS

Delirious Avenues
lit
with the chandelier souls
of infusoria
　　　　—Mina Loy

for my sister, Connie

and in memory of siblings
Norman, Louise, and Sarah

Table of Contents

Tiny Gold Dress

Days so fleet you have to've
seen unruly ones
I do all the time
Someone I soon trust
puts your hand in mine
Just what I'm looking for
Start with the body
and search me
Won't find me sleeping

I dig my six feet
and you stand there in
your tiny gold dress
Can't believe my eyes
Your smile knows
Your ever so slight lisp
Ahead of me in the
opposite direction
Big man alerts me

I shed little bits
of chivalry
I caress like one bereaved
Forethought and hindsight
in the flesh
Peanut shells under bed
Lamp nearby of
fire and roses
Ribbons of smoke sketch
momentarily an orchid

Dispelling Face

Mirror boy mirror girl
Never can you tell
in the mirror world
contradiction from ambiguity
Alliteration of tires at noon
Inconsistencies of the equal
and the functions they suggest
Axis pass through one
dispelling face
The prices she pays in life
I watch through the veil
When she's ready you
know there's no replacement
She signs with a snake
three times of her neck
the communal letter of odium

Reverie comes hard
Sometime granma looks good
Voluptitude that never resolves
Seems always snookered
three feet from the well
Back of the hand
large with veins
Eyelid gleams lavender
out of shadow
Sundry things she
wears at her waist
Hip things to do
in captivity

Room to Sleep

To breathe and measure
all else that lives
Not breathe and risk
the memory you inherit
There is a way, everybody say
the shadow of a branch
in autumn gust, flicks across
her face and imprints it on
the air of my suspirations

Once the detective who
can find your guitar
Now I weave up Avenue A
abstracted in the vision
of her bushy eyebrows
Her eyes offer room to sleep

Only so tall, it is Fall
Hand deep in coals
left by careless sparks
Night lengthens to blow
on them with dreams
I invent her radiance
Exaggeration is slight
Identify her straight stride
Sun at her back
A world away

Daredevils

I go outside in
early summer dawn
if what I hear there
appeals to me
The air stirs I
don't say it's cool
Heat is what you wear
and great heat
is small apparel
Blow desert sand
off her hand
disturbed from
the lair it provides
deep-digging creatures
Look of shock as air
rolls around her
arms and collarbone
She dances, conquer
by conjure, clapping
of waves chest high
Applause from sidewalk
Recipient registers with
close-lipped smile
in no direction
Magic her vocabulary
with other myths of
commerce and self-respect
Asphalt where daredevils wait
Lights timed to eternity

Overhang

Overhang at midday a respite
Blood stands out on concrete
Steer your great big shapely feet aside
Lookers on overhear password imperfectly
Aftermath of a rout
Identify who is off target
A beautiful woman and the hideous
Advise to stamp out burning heart
Her tan palm earth brown lines
of fortune of life of heartlessness
Don't know what's tomorrow
Damaged by survival
begins where it ends

Hubbub stars taxi man
Five year girl of angelic ebony
Forehead broad shiny globe
Sun begins to rust
on momma's slim waist
You are built for gold paved streets
where I have never been
Cheap to grant victory
Catastrophe rinses cleaner

Across the street across the wall
Backyard next to bus stop
Litter and noise
Page turns in gust
turns back under hand
Rather know

Crepe

for George Schneeman

Empty the city
of its right- handed
Cold measures wall
for crepe
I am transported
the same old way
Heartache at my heels
Expensive cars
parked badly
wall off trees
Wind unrelenting
for a hundred feet
Where those who
out of my
affection ascend
I attempt
to climb in
their wake
I don't know
the doorman
Nor the floor
I have only
your name

It comes to pass
Nothing to render
shadows with
Head bends in

foyer
Something tells me
Look through
glass door:
Wet tissues
in the wind

Black Lapel

I touch I stay
The glass empties
You notice so little
Remember later
Moral anergy
This round's on me

Bathed mauve in bathos
Crowd meanders
with a purpose
Disappointment
makes me tipsy
Stars poke out of
infinite black lapel
I return to your eyes
Brows no longer soothe
Delusions enter
discourteously
Ha-ha ha-ha ha ha

Despite Murder

She deserves better by someone
Desire for the worst to happen
Feel like she really join
communal genius of misery
Resist entering because of the bricks
In this heat you've got a point
Outdoor weather suits your clothes
Streetlights gold against
turquoise horizon after
a mean sun disappears
Bunch of girls mosies off
in search of the offensive

In the day they called me Lucky
Problems were beginning
even as countless others were
not resolved despite murder
She left me uptown and
I came down with my pants
over my head walking backwards
Assured of glory like
her other million fools

Naked Fingers

Premonitions rise as body does
Back on dry land
With what to mingle distress
Sources of light unstable
Remove petals of metallic pink
with naked fingers
Out the window ratty tree top
blows free of leaves
Dress to ward off
wind and welshers
Activity in hair
Novel ways of cold
in a village of mani-pedi
Do not trust the assessors

If particles obey words
The carpet bears flowers
on rainy days
My eyes are dry
Glance inappropriate
Can we somehow change
position inseparably
Door with steps missing

I find no one else
Well, a monologue then
Questions about parting
Firm grasp abrupted
Scent attaches to a name

Legs wrapped in sheets of water
Hands that caress know
the price of invasion
Glove in the gutter
starched by tires
grasps a necklace
Which windows are lit changes
Goodbye to the moon
Leave there forever
First cry

You Can't Tell

You move a long
long way
You mispronounce
your own name
You naturalize
the void where
care have been taken

You rattle the
knives in a drawer
You appear to
be looking for rope

In retrospect you
can't tell will
it be today
Which things in mind
are the ones you do

To suggest there
be a wind
There already is
The way you move

In Your Waking Life

Shoe falls in hospital
Tableau when the curtain parts
Like specters the healthy
approach and pass
A dream of repose which
in your waking life
you remember as confusions
Of crazy arms with billowing drape
Voice with wind through blinds
To get it you have to
be here and I'm not

But now the woman is
and refreshing questions
You have ten dollars
more than you thought
Curtains around legs
flag and reveal
An eggish sunlight
So many sorts of
pelvic formfiture
with backlit details
And there on the margins
in the middle of the street
as if talking to myself
A song

To You For By

Somebody somewhere
couldn't say nothing
'til I call myself self
Choice profile in
the crosswalk an
encounter again
with wonder
Something shows
of all that can
contain anger
Just as cocoa
butter wipes off
brown from clean skin
Send for yesterday
yesterday, clock
the race of particles
through the tomb
that surrounds
your marketplace
with hecklers

What you suppose
recklessness calls
to you for by
name in a
private language
It shunts you to
thoughts more precious
than memory

Swipe your card
Descend the steps
and incise the crowd
to undercut this
your epiphany
Subway platform
induce such
civilities as are silent
After the first
hundred there's
nobody else around
Safe now to touch
small faces with oils

Worth More Alive

Alone you are not querulous
Alone discomfort is
insensible to the hybrid
Your pose today: perfidy
Yet blossoms attach to
the reflective black glow
of your eyes in twilight
Absence holds things together
And I do not follow you

Bursting with fertile stems
Cafeteria windows bask
and make compelling
Skin of a hip in motion
Extended fingers twist
bills for a ready count
Retract with essential ballet
Her child next to her wayward
But then beauty has
its drawbacks

Face overwhelmed by attention
Camera turns her statement
into rising lilt of a question
Hand clasps an elbow
Barrette catches light
Attempts at defilement
shore up her restlessness
Purity in the inconstant

nature of things
Smallest box within boxes
Breeze plays with hair
Senses feel less funny
Being always with someone
asks few of these questions
Unshoddy is worth more alive
Pretend to need help
Last one of all to know
the end of ministrations

The Urge

Miss all the time
Keys of sterling silver
Can't find the door
Anthem ends and you
are singing alone
Lift your cheek from
the metal you tread
Step of a burglar

Street retards ardor
Substitution of
stellar streetlamps
Door gone the way of ice
No way heat doesn't
blast, there could
be smoke any minute

I recall an unusual
way to count her fingers
without using my own
Dark enough under the tree
Silhouettes two into one
Overlapping in arrest
Seen on the move because
the urge to stop is
hosed off this sidewalk

Enlighten the amateur
There's no stopping now

So many buzzers
without names
Doors without
distinguishing marks
Just like they say

On Turbulence

Those who listen
make their way
among your friends
Incomprehension
deploys elbow
to elbow
Railing cools
under my hand
Streetlights
multiply shadows
Preliminary lift
on turbulence
Ever ready to fly
as if high above
wooded hills
A passionate
exchange out
of memory
Uncontainable
synergy
Legs hair face breasts
all overlap
Sweat pools in navel
Air moves again
its observations
concluded
Mercy, mercy
the clouds are bruisers
Nobody knows
Nobody will

Off the Curb

Overwhelmed by adequacy
Lower lip salient
Body language
of apostrophes
The hard head
buttress against
the ooze of
plenitude
I ask for three cards
Now I know
I can fly
and give my
life to reality

If I say it
so poignantly
I tell a lie
Every step like
off the curb
Inured to
the jarring
The space around
me exceeds
the formulae
I feel it in
the arms I wrap
it like a person in

Only to Pry

Except it isn't silent
More droplet than drop
this rain strains its name
to visualize tinnitus
Choose most repellent coat
Go where nearby women
shelter in wait of bus
Whisper the tonality
and draw you near
What might I hear as
one slips in exit door

To think is to see
I invite you and
you only to pry
Sight I wear
like a poncho
Contemplation
inhales smoke
Comfort in turmoil
To record posture in youth
What foot traffic is for
To identify you
and only you

You lean forward to laugh
Your face never
repeats an expression

Tired you appear
less than your age
You are beyond you
and always in my path

Such Angels

Headland behind me
All the suspicions
that drain heaven
Has no taste, snow
but aftertaste of lanolin
protects such angels as fly
Look for something orange
Instead see a light
There will be smoke

By far the most radiant
heap of grime
Narrowed byways
Each step succeeded
by splatter
Seems more and more often
that darkness descends
Without wind I prefer it

Sidewalks are I know
very large rooms
To circle the room
I need a partner
Turns out the accent
is French french
I take her hand in mine
She begins to dance

Time is ripe, put that
down for a second

Around us lights on
the inside are the outside
What about our clothing
Our scarves begin
an intimacy
An hour sooner or later
Everything that happens
The ones we abandon

Deep and Wary

Frame of mind with haze
where dreams die
Ones that don't
are heartbroken dreams
Birds of night bust
the pollen nut
tree to tree
Generate O generate
midriffs that thirteen
years from now
are bared

You get loose and
you get away
Tonight stepping good
A sprinter's walk
The music of what
you feel gutters out
No one around
to be in concert with
Finis

Young brown face
Square, eyes set deep
and wary, her nose
long straight and broad
She has someplace to go
She has someone to be
She finds out
a small and equal
cost of hope

Through the Climates

Wobbly as her rotation is
Don't be abused
of the notion
Skirt short lips
fire orange on brown
Eyes that take you
through the climates
Make a pothole
beautiful and watch
snow fall
Her step is sure
Scarf blows
four ways in one
Gets a little nutty
A music that meets
the demands of
as little light
as there is

Flat Swing

Lie on arrival then
we outta here
Just shiver in the
thick hide of mirth
She as ever radiant
Blemished cheeks of
windswept shape
Recipe for expulsion
Your unnatural force
and a flat swing
marry recklessness
Stare right through
someone else's dream
Zoom in on deadend street
any girl'd lie to get off
Slowly fold in umbrage
At first she looks lost
Big sexy legs
See her then don't
then see her again
the very last time

Ripple

If I only remember
a single thing
Catastrophe up close
too many, too cheap
Erotic pinnacles
after all pedestrian
Why not the face none
too pretty, vibrant eyes
One wonders how dark
brown can be and
burnish rose on a cheekbone
She knows what I see
She knows I am thorough

Where was it, time
rolls into the playground
Yes, it was the Church Avenue
platform, Saturday
Light jacket a plus
I who no longer feel
white faces, without
advantage my license
I attract faces with
courtesy of notice
Means little to her
while she talks on
Bluetooth ear bud
hid by her weave

Ambient Ululations

Come to this
Pedestrians whose language
I maul pause to hear
my prevarications
They needn't hide the desire
for a different liberty
Pavement mapped with stains
in every direction
Ambient ululations
You and I wrapped in stripes
and dots of attention
Colors on the tribal side
Behavior of ghosts
Keep one hand wide open

Rain falls like smoke
Lightning fluoresces
Her long legs flash icily
Plash reaches her knee
I remain standing
but I teeter
My call goes out
Comes back, only
words is all

To the Touch

Just try to get in
Greeted by emptiness
Girls lean against trees
were there trees
So silent I doubt audition
There is someone
to help you
Firm to the eye
Velour to the touch

A cord to pull
to slow my fall
Toss pillow to reserve
table in corner
Breathe candle's leavings
More than one ocean
abounds as before
Member's card lights the tracks

Depot of lightning
Breath plays tricks
Sconce with translucent
ribs nests in bunker
Shadow darkens even more
one side of your thigh
A fixture is moving
Expensive dizziness
Aphorism in foreign tongue
Now I belong
my color changes
Careless, careless moon

Ultimate Word

Your silhouette against the window
Your knowledge and impudence
Your body emits an ambiguous you
You glamorize that deficit

My admiration sets its standards
Distrust I don't share
of sentiment
Denial enlivens it

Nothing objective pertains
You a sovereign
Riches of the world
you deserve and don't taste

Grave won't stay clean
Rusted foliage of pine
Incised markings stained
by weathers and resin
Beloved the ultimate word

Is the Place

Baby never cries
Over there is the place
for a moon
A watertower
and its planets
My tongue gets dry
while they are asleep
on my feet
Baby will hardly
remember my face

Loath to exercise
standard sense
Out of order suits me
Which hand I extend
Like touching oily beads
They brush aside and
there is the image
of you only

Silhouette

for Heaven C. (1995-1995)

Heaven a name
Not a place you get to
Wear the garment wet
Let me tell you something
about how you breathe
I spare descriptions

Protocol of false starts
Economical casket
An infant aflame and
then off with if not
off to your name
Incommensurate memory
It all ensues without you
Why is that a lesson

2

You are incapable
There are hands many hands
to lift your head and
fan where you burn
Whomever satisfaction
does not humiliate

3

Born with a profile
Silhouette cut from
caramel crêpe

Death mask vitiates
If it turns out to
be a place, why, there's
no one better suited

Own Two

You got to keep them
portents in their place
Unsettled by woe and
savoring chatter
Two or three inebriated
women fall past
me in space

The pill is gravity
It arrives from
across the seaboard
Tethered here at
the Winthrop stop
She lifts both
infant and stroller
over the turnstile
with her own two hands
She lowers them
like a tray of drinks
She doesn't want to sit
She takes up room
Babymomma and Lateisha

If she push up
on her arms and
raise her head
to see at two months
If she recognize
her name at four

The Edge Off

Buildings don't have wings
in the place where
she spreads hers over
rivulets across
the sidewalk's slope
A bit unthorough
in the trough, did you
water down risk
to the shape in smoke of
the dangerous and the naïve
Fleece goes with a wisp
but not with her

She has the money
and when she does it
she does it with a knife
Winter sundown hour
Floral drapes blur
the edge off natural light
Skirt wraps one hip
by the window
Confident now

Just the Song

Without a single word
Exit the wrong room
Take the stairs down
Arms wrap around me
Fold me through
the bars of a cell
No music but voices
I find something out
It will never live again
on the breath of dames

It begins as a sanctuary
Free to strip to nothing
Just the song for you

Arrows in Sand

Cold wind with complaisance
Not to see the points of it
Vegetarian crocodiles in my dream
The castanets I take off to eat
What makes me feel this way
The moment arrives for saying

Call it evocation
How easy to repeat
Cameroon Cameroon
In such heat
my tremor departs
My senses drowse
Reason has vapors
The crocodiles are mating
No soundtrack, no strings

What call your garment
Wind cuts arrows in sand
Last body standing
Who are you meets
who you are
By your leave
my ship sets sail
At what price defend
hope against ventilation
What share of sandstorm
What tide wash
bodies ashore

Lip Read

Take into consideration
the broken route run by wind
Engage the sidewalk as
dance floor for whom
I ever attend to
I insist to be bidden
The short unfiltered one
notes the call
Progress to decay
through blossoms
She reacts to my appearance
with sympathy
Another verse of
the unrequited

But the light is harsh
Lunch in hand
with shade so spotty
Perfect skin is rare
It arrives a newborn
and departs in family arms
Cheeks of an amphibian
to be shaped by the past

The train I miss
throbs below ground
Footfalls lessen, lip-
read goodbyes
Of all the traffic laws

to observe, cimarron
red car parks in the
pyramidal glow of
navel oranges
The hand that inspects
is not in mine
They call it raincoat
Leg dries matte brown
Press breast against stone
Ditty in a minor key
I hear and am healed

So Real

One of these days
you begin to cherish
the landmark
you see so easily
By the window
memorabilia
The woman the cat
Roil with transience
which incontrovertibly
stagnates, its fossil
the overlapping frets
Ashes cold are shrines
Breathe life into them
Warmth to spare
Offer incense fruits
exquisite pewter
Power, breath, power
All in my dreams
Everything so real
Clothes more colorful
Drinks so cheap

Large in Smoke

Branches the only
moving things
Reflections fix to
window glass
the whole block long
Hear but do not listen

Cunning is as
silent does
Coarsens what is
writ large in smoke
Sky somewhat rustles

Deluxe interiors
Excess of instruments
Chrome the random cursive
of parking regulations
Comfort does just fine
when not employed

Dual exhausts for
expulsion of logic

Platinum

The loudmouths are functional
Wind turns hawk some
Sidewalk rolls up like nothing

I wonder at platinum gray
where sky actually shows
I hear only the steam

of my own ears at rest
Melanchomic melody
Laconic lyrics afloat

I know the language
Hushed strokes of ink

The Lacuna

Underfoot the fragments
The totem and fetish
Coming mad real

Beating fast all chambers
Vulva opens lips brown
Touches me with herself

Her occupancy registers
That's where it's possible
to slake the lacuna

Delirium slits the eyes
Blonde fall, nose glistens broad
I'm for the features

And what am I not
Window of restraint
As if I would be spent

Sane over easy
Pink palms, mauve nails
In the future those

without a future

Her Ground

Early for the password
Big street quiet
passes for order
Wind mocks my whosies
Her name rhymes
depending on which name
Many scratch their heads
and unload her own
intensity on her

Too late for pastorale
All the blue mouths
in the jungle go mute
All the horns in the
rainforest play microtones
The desert is where
your body reappears

Here where bus routes
distinguish among you
Rebels outlaws mistakes
Savant'll be the end of me
Where it happens
is not any somewhere
My labyrinths and
then I am sailing
Evaporate that propels me
Waves and swells

between cars
Name a storm for her
She holds her ground
lodged in the world

Random Swimmers

Bed gets tight with floor
Darkness denies
sculpting of sheets
What song is this
Ceiling sets tempo
Pillow empty, still warm
Footstep so light
Be kind to her, night

Telescope trains on skirt
I play a busy out-theme
Hoofers and heifers
Return me to my sleep
I dream that I cooly
do not want the light
Sleep in an amusement park
A sock of sand
in the bass drum
Random swimmers
and water a stage
Hello hello, go
ahead now, river
and talk in my sleep

Walk down the street
dodging rafts
Prizes of the sea
tiding in
Tight wet jeans
for the mermaid

Wind-tossed horizon
for a figment
Rolling gait of a sailor
on a marked deck of cards

Crazy Arms

Crazy arms from backseat
window as it pulls away
Interior darkness a puzzle
Street luminous with lamps
and flashes off loopy earrings
Tracers of color slide
down rear window
It gets smaller, makes a turn
Stymies pursuit of desire

Maybe your ancestors
Not mine
She remains, car stationary
Rear door this side opens
She extends nothing
Draws you in

2

The sky attempts
an unforetold clemency
Illumination of her palette
Hair bleached by glare
where black sheens
Action profile, high forehead
High breasts, gaze high
Flaws sublime
And I one who
tires of looking
like who I am

Ambient, Some

Where, how survive the storm
Dove purls on railing
newly bare of snow
Wind doubling in volume
Fracture haunts sidewalk
Frigidly wet or viscously frozen
Sun not to speak of
Just taking the bait
smarter than who keep
body and fool together
Gun in the drawers
Sounds ambient, some
of them trouble
Tears bleed from wind
Faces blur and just
the same I see them

By Recall

I won't find out
No one comes back for it
I wake up any place any time
I enjoy a hazy moment or so
Ceiling collaborates when it flies
away from stubborn trash
in back city

I can do better than that
I have cleansing resources
scathed some by recall
When I clearly see
without belief
Gracious aging face
beside herself with sleep
How a caress adds to history
Of flesh chief is wonder

Can Hush

Rocking gait as rain pelts
Trousers weigh, heart decompresses
toward the surface
Precipitate ghosts, the seaward sky
Those who plunge in coming home
I am ashamed of the umbrella

Wet finger of wind
Curl pastes to her forehead
Such won't let me die
You have to look up
to your body
It can hush

Splatter's all the sound
The precipitants melting
Flood of those passed passing
My wet feet alive
Sewer collects its storm
Light changes for
half-blinded drivers
Like a funeral cortege
They all turn right

Rain, Boy

When floodlights impair
Ample darkness confound
She has a handle on
public dishabille in
contrast to the blond
decay of leaves
My surrender
is conditional
Zephyr's chilly reprise
Close brush with significance
that beast I
forget the name

Rain, boy, beating
on those windowpanes
Umbrella decked with
skull and bones
Hips in a crouch
Wavelengths across
Stoop light lost
in reflection
Her face completes
an annunciation
Close around
wings beat
Shelter, one supposes
opens out, doors in

Many Duets

Galleries where shots
were silent
Cathedrals of raunch
Stage set with
men's room
How many duets
extinguish on
accumulated air
Forgiveness built
on distrust and
disordered prism
of memories
Countless eggs thrown
out of bepeopled drabness
What looks best
to me blinds you
eminence aside
Read fortune in
handbills as they swirl
There is license in
the color of that lip
of those thighs
All of it on loan
Long as you know
your way around

Her Elbow Exactly

All I ever wanted
Last look at your face
Peril at great remove
Discipline asserts
palms up, parallel
to the world
Sleight of mind

Song around the town
Theater of *savoir*
Rhythm of polished flaws
Misstep with grace
on virgin subway
Wind of arrival
causes cling
Goddess on the platform
Don't stare, stanchion
at her elbow exactly
where the door opens
Bad manners cross
her purpose, she stands
No special care

Correct the Air

There are friendships
that resemble curiosity
There are friendships
that dissemble equality
There are friendships of
no standards at all
Correct the air that
stands here drowned
Kiss of amelioration
undoes a man's esteem
Forget the judgment
implied by rags
hanging from trees
Knowledge isn't
a meaningful word
but as a bubble
it will do

Betrays Nothing

Dignify her comeuppance
with lowered voice
with myth with backbone
Offer semblance of longing
in arbitrary words
Her indolence the dance
of contingencies
She swipes the glass
off the table and
tilts back her head
If the wits about me
are indeed mine

Makeup betrays nothing
Her expression pleasant
but interminably fixed
She is jealous of her voice
It is hard to share
now it is the one she wants
Her grip on the napkin
too tight for drying lips
The same lips part
and I believe her

Cloud That Breaks

Must have the living
to call it a place
Must have a location
to experience the wait
The ups and downs
separate me from memory
Idleness of uncertain kind
You know what you are not
Belief in the nonapparent
The table of cloud
that breaks my fall
City reflects glow of skin
Naked elbow against
sleeve of coat
Door jiggles with draft
Eye on the wobbly flame
Wick glows, smoke dances
Then, nowhere it is

Who's Left

Doll's in love
Dust everywhere
Guy with a crashbar
Curtains sop a puddle
Chair is gone
Look who's left
So much gets flossy
and ill in the ghetto
You can tell by an odor
A big pipe I mean big
Comforts are invented
No regard for solid colors
Makes you aware
of speculation
Silver where most often
a gene would have indigo
Mismatched cutlery
Flawless blades discarded
Newport filter
after you sit on it
Something almost daylike
Change makes way
for changes
That ring veiny red
all the lightless time
No bones define your hand
It turns away my eyes

Of Stray Dogs

Ghosts of stray dogs
pad out the theater
I say to Skipper
Where'd they take
the girl in the shower
They cut off the water
he says
I ask the same of Roman
who is fixated
Curtain caught on fire
but it was beaded with
shampooey droplets
he says
I saved you some steam
I look askance like
he takes his momma's name
So instead of heading off
as a trio to Korea
I walk away with
a direction but no
visible means
of destination

Hundred Bullet Toast

I return improbably soon
First rays brighten dust
Sounds I cannot make
get made themselves
Breath visible on cold steel
Framed ailanthus crown sways
in the wake of delivery
Language seems once to
have been old
Last dream punctuated
by the changing color
of one person's skin
and the vision
is not repeated

What are you looking for
in the way of....
Windows all glow of rust
Strobe by eastern sky
Lives that never sleep
No one looks waify
Lips carved of cherry
Hundred bullet toast
He says "My darling"
Coffee wash it clean
Feeling most hid
Trunks of my heart

Orange highlights begin
Cold as December is

Witness leaves no prints
Trees fit for a park
I walk under
Blistering words
made cool

An Idol

Noise she's making
tells me hide the roses
Allay her with rubber
snake out of Brooklyn
Climb her stoop
in wilderness
Follow instructions
Drum fingertips
on her door
I magnify
the small blunder
Hand holds out scarf
Its softness distracts
What to do with
the cigarette
Without caution it
happens, so successfully
myself keeps up, just
Curves so wide
in Flatlands
Legs that
an idol make

The Impediments

Flimsy shift, a gust
Story in progress
not yet put to bed
Impalpable but still rain
Eyeful with a snoot full
Quill-like eruptions
on her umbrella
You're the one said
"Good morning"
Discard propriety
like a maidenhead
Skeptical driver
unusually small cab
Soundless departure
So let us not return
to the impediments
Pardon me a second
My shoe is gripped
by something
in the pavement
Funny how I
notice these things

Lip Print

Derangement of ventilation
Breathless mounts the bus
All we who notice
The savant the untrustworthy
the stained with heat
Why do I supplicate
when her skirt hugs

She weaves without jostle
through inhospitable standees
Lip print on sip lid
Stimulates herself
like *chez soi*
Coffee breath with pardons
Avenues by fast

Pink-on-brown stripe
from shoulder strap
Ear buds, R&B head bob
Necessity and freedom
Tall words for attraction
One time seen
The bus kneels

Part of Your Skin

What have you done now
Recruited by brightness
Away with you
I gather up the folded
towels in your wake
All kidding aside

How do you think
I describe you
The skirt that is
part of your skin
The ankle wrapped
around a hand

Lips a wind shaves
Redress about to explode
You float nearby
Lamplight reaches out
to tether you to lingerie
You have fewer choices
than you know
and I value no secret

To Transit Its Permit

Lose track of the ones
you see in offtime too
The lights of day use
their own death as
a weapon, so much
time wasted in relief
Liquid sky clears to
translucent amber
to vindicate me
Those who sit
bound the footpath
and for every impediment
to transit its permit
Pass a vision in brown
Very long feet sprayed
with flawless skin
and that smits me
When you come to
the embankment stick
to the part you can see
Contemplate remorse
which belongs to no one
and spare my peers

Return the Chain

Theme music fades
That's what the din
sounds like to
the director
When I'm through
watching I return
the chain to
the right counter
Sidewalk material
again the street
confirms me
Something to look
into something strong

I cannot fulfill
helplessness with
you in mind
There're problems yes
The warrant
The bargain
The necessity to
step to the side
My face is saved by
unbroken stride

The Last Thing

I may be bound to depths
There's only one heaven
if you go there twice
Celestial streetlamps
the last Keds hang from
I stretch to reach
Nothing doing
Forbidden things leave
their brand on my residence
Body if you will
Impels me to postulate
a friction less than
thigh against thigh
The last thing to do
is to wrong
This sidewalk's part
of the trail
Twilight connects some dots
Successions of gravity echo
My every last step

Your Palate

What other face
can be so indifferent
What other voice a universe
No blanket
to the policy
Make room for her
dangling costume

You sit messily
with wrong people
Cheap decor a wonder
Request a more
succinct menu
Urchins from
the four elements
Soup of
recantation
Dessert on wings
Aromas expand to
explode on
your palate
Like your very
last words

Able to Tell

Madrigal of torpor pass me over
Accustomed to vigor I play with the world
Separate salvage from souvenirs
It is a place seldom green and
then in the context of yellow
Through windows specked with flakes
I see you sit on the aisle facing forward
This is not self-determination
This is a moment

What happens next is nothing yet
Wash of bus acceleration
moves hair aggressively
Situation all trundled up
She moves quickly to a seat
she doesn't have to share
Window rolls shrunken away
I have a long block to go

Come down come down little white things
You will be able to tell where I go
The heels are barely worn
and there is no tread

On the Level

Please don't go
There are things
you don't know
Make believe love
is street talk
Intimate
the way I die
Point out highlights
Landscape of her body
Treehouse in her hair
She dives and loses
the suit you never
believe she wears
She's on the level

If only on weekends
Presentiment and
presentation
I conclude with your leg
Squint of amusement
in your small eyes
You assert an
intention to know
Blacker than brown
finger casts shadow
of hanged man
In her dream I
sleep or is it die

Hear Right

Hand print on mirror
Dust where only
dust leaves behind
Cigarette odor stain
Blouse shines amid dimness
Finger impresses crumbs
Response all miscued
Turns on the lamp
They say harmony resigns
Now for a sip
The glass secures light
and lets it loose
in nearby corners
Her lips begin
the summary
Ambient sound augments
Cigarette falls
faster than ash
Feet shuffle
under chairs
You hear right
The last door down
the last hall
The one you want

Submarine Midnight

Some gladden
at the sight
The form the
pants fit
Eyes fit the nose
As alert a walk
as can still glide
For hours after I
can enjoy no one else
Wander here where
I wish was
my destination
Alberta Clipper
ranges past distress
Snow falls steadily
I slip readily
from admiration to
submarine midnight
I want youth
I want them to go
by in front of me
To remind me:
You never know

Befits

First I enjoy your attention
and let go of it now
I take your fear of
the monster personally
You fall in love
The mouth of the
loved one opens
and hollers "Fire!"

Your voice drowns
out in this town
There is the Up and
the Down and there
are the Sides naturally
Your word is your
liability even as it
rebukes pain for its
pretension to blessing

Some brisk so
the hoodie's up
Young young boy toddles
behind, steps on cracks
His momma wears tight
to feel not alone
Resentment without
revenge for makeup
She text somebody
right now and dish

I pass women in a
universe of covered heads
The light is grayish
blue and against it
her brown befits
one glorious face
My sentiment, my
sentiments fail
because, accurate
they're at fault

They harmonize with
these few bars
and will confound
you as long as you sing
of forty-year old
voluptuousness
She listens carelessly
as I disappear into
such a hungry
feeling and daylight
on my hand as I wake
to her red wig and
her local gown

The One

When the moon
begins its fall
You'll be the one

A little bit of
clothing, lipstick stain
Come apart this way

Daunt or undaunt
You straighten your seams
It's all trip to you

and you arrive too soon
The only way 'round
your past is away

Face the timetable
A little past noon
Tell them don't wait

Inside the Moon

Spell your name uniquely
To see your clothes
is to see your body
All burdened and unrighteous
Your adversary is smithereens
A river called by music
Something to tap into
when you feel hokey haute

The look of a satin doll
Sweet forget-about-it
I see the bounded spell
of her face it comes
out at night
Violet in the sheen
I never want the earth
to be inside the moon

She locks up her hair
Water on both sides
A bridge too close
Turns the light up
on that corner to
fill the ville with scent
No more li'l bitty baby
Corner of Garvey and Amazon
A millionaire buys less
The science it takes
Infinite infinite particles
The beatings of the heart

Unfurnished

With a fresh and
odd motivation
All convictions amend
Lead desire from peril
Wait for midnight's erasure
of the Empire's lighted tip
Then feel your way by
wet to the touch

Reality remands you
Partitions of smoke
River of dust motes
I a tributary
furnished with
myriad options
for the credulous
No grace to be lost

From what store comes
calm after gunshots
Toothy smiles when
the subject is hair
Lamp each end of bar
Here a backless halter
There a jacket over nothing
Shame it's all smokeless

Pardon the starless, cloudless
sky, moon some fraction

Retro-fitted solitude around
Cleavage keeps peace
A bounce in the step

Start of the Ball

Here at the start of the ball
Carousel of patent leather on toes
In the still center a camera shines
No one I mean no one
wears a mask or pink
The cry out loud of disbelief
It's the lyric of deciding
to have your own say
Spades in the room
wait to be called
I believe fetters are real

To wrap me inside my body
My mind has properties so distant
Not from neglect do
squatters warm there
Ground under my body attaches
me to itself, when I soar
my intent is to offend it
I learn defiance from textures
of a body's surface, silence flows
through the wall at which gravity ends

As I Might

Don't tell the whole story
You like a serious ellipse
Laugh when you measure it
Don't dig on gibberish
Farther and farther afield
punch out a niche
to foot the bill
At the root of it all
a woman you dream real
Before you sit down
she brushes off the step
Comes along a judge
Wonder where is that
gambling man gone to
Everybody knows where I am
The cave wraps around
At ease with the stranger's shadow
Tell it as I might
Collection of bits and pieces
Ending on-the-move in
replications of a present
Who's to say more

Shadows This Long

Kind of pre-formed glow
Silhouette built where
buildings will be
How long before you
first use your voice
Gray phase achieves
its impermanence
What day begins in
clarity I cleave to

Glare dances ribbons
Day rises on an elbow
Crepuscular adage that
shadows this long have life
I welcome them among us
who have ones of our own
Who turn from nocturnal
music with blank memory

If I say hello
your attention is obliged
So little else answers
Footsteps in a crowd
ask and ask
At least one be a
prima donna and
sebaceous perfumes abate

So must I vie
A woman with turn

and I turn
Turquoise chunk of wood
holds down the news
Daybreak salsa Bustelo scent
You who are conditional
You who immerse
And I emerge

Dances in Airshaft

Music tinny and distant
The suppliant lingers outside
until the strip search ends
The enforcer capitulates
details of squalor
Everything as it
isn't known to be

The tee-shirt damply clings
yet feels of coolness
Nothing in tropical night
prepares you for the flashes
The grace note is static

Clothesline dances in airshaft
Scenes of guarded liveliness
Muffled voice of a girl
on her phone by window
Couple dressed special
leaves footsteps on stairs
Old man hums and
cuts his bid by half

John Godfrey was born in 1945, in Massena, N.Y.
He took degrees at Princeton and Columbia.
He has published a dozen books and chapbooks of poems.
He has lived in Manhattan's East Village since the 1960s.
He is a retired RN Clinician in HIV/AIDS.

Books by John Godfrey

26 Poems (Adventures in Poetry, 1971)

Three Poems (Bouwerie Editions, 1973)

Music of the Curbs (Adventures in Poetry, 1976)

Dabble: Poems 1966–1980 (Full Court Press, 1982)

Where the Weather Suits My Clothes (Z Press, 1984)

Midnight On Your Left (The Figures, 1988)

Push the Mule (The Figures, 2001)

Private Lemonade (Adventures in Poetry, 2003)

City of Corners (Wave Books, 2008)

Singles and Fives (Fewer and Further, 2012)